THE ULTIMATE GUIDE TO
WEDDING MUSIC

LYRICS FOR 100
POPULAR WEDDING SONGS

Lyrics For 100 Popular Wedding Songs

THE FOLLOWING PAGES CONTAIN THE LYRICS to 100 of the most popular songs for weddings. Since weddings are so special, it is sometimes the words alone that encourage you to choose one song over another. Sit back and enjoy the beautiful sentiment found in the following songs.

LYRICS FOR 100 POPULAR WEDDING SONGS

LYRICS FOR 100 POPULAR WEDDING SONGS

LYRICS FOR 100 POPULAR WEDDING SONGS

LYRICS FOR 100 POPULAR WEDDING SONGS

AFTER ALL

(Love Theme from *Chances Are*)

Well, here we are again
I guess it must be fate
We've tried it on our own
But deep inside we've known
We'd be back to set things straight

I still remember when
Your kiss was so brand new
Every memory repeats
Every step I take retreats
Every journey always brings me back to you

Chorus:
After all the stops and starts
We keep coming back to these two hearts
Two angels who've been rescued from the fall
After all that we've been through
It all comes down to me and you
I guess it's meant to be
Forever you and me, after all

When love is truly right
(this time it's truly right)
It lives from year to year
It changes as it goes
And on the way it grows
But it never disappears

(Chorus)

Always just beyond my touch
You know I needed you so much
After all, what else is living for?

Words & Music by Dean Pitchford and Tom Snow

All I Do Is Dream Of You

All I do is dream of you the whole night through
With the dawn, I still go on dreamin' of you

You're every thought, you're everything,
You're every song I ever sing
Summer, winter, autumn an' spring!

And were there more than 24 hours a day
They'd be spent in sweet content dreamin' away

When skies are gray, skies are blue
Morning, noon an' nighttime too
All I do the whole day through is dream of you!

And were there more than 24 hours a day
They'd be spent in sweet content dreamin' away

When skies are gray, skies are blue
Morning, noon an' nighttime too
All I do the whole day through is dream of you!

Words by Arthur Freed, Music by Nacio Herb Brown

All I Ever Need Is You

Sometimes when I'm down and all alone
Just like a child without a home.
The love you give me keeps me hangin' on
Oh honey, All I ever need is you

You're my first love, you're my last,
You're my future, you're my past.
And loving you is all I ask.
Honey, all I ever need Is you

Winters come and they go,
And we watch the melting snow.
Sure as summer follows spring,
All the things you do give me a reason
To build my world around you

Some men follow rainbows
Some men search for silver
Some for gold
I have found my treasure in your soul

Without love I'd never find the way
Through ups and downs of ev'ry single day
I won't sleep at night until you say
My honey, all I ever need Is you

Words & Music by Jimmy Holiday and Eddie Reeves

ALL I HAVE

You can say you love me
And I believe that's true
Trusting you is easy
'Cause I believe in you
There is nothing I would miss
As long as we're in love like this

Chorus:
All I have
Is all I need
And it all comes down to you and me
How far away this world becomes
In the harbor of each other's arms.

I feel like I've known you forever and ever,
Baby that's how close we are
Right here with you is where
My life has come together,
And where love has filled my heart.
You know I'd go anywhere
As long as I had you to care.

(Chorus)

Ooh, and with the love you bring.
I never want for anything.
I found what I've been searching for
In you.

Words & Music by Beth Nielsen Chapman

ALL THE MAN THAT I NEED

I used to cry myself to sleep at night
But that was all before he came
I thought that love has to hurt to turn out right,
But now he's here, Its not the same
Its not the same

Chorus:
He fills me up.
He gives me love
More love then I've ever seen.
He's all I've got
He's all I've got in this world
But he's all the man that I'll ever need

And in the morning when I kiss his eyes
He takes me down,
He rocks me slow

And in the evening when the moon is high,
He holds me close
And won't let go
He won't let go

(Chorus)

Words by Dean Pitchford, Music by Michael Gore

All The Things You Are

Time and again I've longed for adventure,
Something to make my heart beat the faster.
What did I long for? I never really knew.
Finding your love I've found my adventure,
Touching your hand, my heart beats the faster,
All that I want in all of this world is you.

Chorus:
You are the promised kiss of springtime
That makes the lonely winter seem long.
You are the breathless hush of evening
That trembles on the brink of a lovely song.
You are the angel glow that lights a star,
The dearest things I know are what you are.
Some day my happy arms will hold you,
And some day I'll know that moment divine,
When all the things you are, are mine!

Words & Music by Oscar Hammerstein III and Jerome Kern

All Through
The Night

All through the night
I'll be awake and I'll be with you
All through the night
This precious time when time is new
Oh, all through the night today
Knowing that we feel the same without saying

Chorus:
We have no past we won't reach back
Keep with me forward all through the night
And once we start the meter clicks
And it goes running all through the night
Until it ends there is no end

All through the night
stray cat is crying so stray cat sings back
All through the night
They have forgotten what by day they lack
Oh under those white street lamps
There is a little chance they may see

(Chorus)

Oh the sleep in your eyes is enough
Let me be there let me stay there awhile

(Chorus)

Keep with me forward all through the night
And once we start the meter clicks
And it goes running all through the night
Until it ends there is no end

Words & Music by Jules Shear

ALWAYS

Girl, you are to me
All that a woman should be
And I dedicate my life to you always

A love like yours is rare;
It must have been sent from up above.
And I know you'll stay this way for always

And we both know
That our love will grow
And forever, it will be
You and me.

Ooh, you're like the sun,
Chasing all the rain away.
When you come around, you bring brighter days.

You're the perfect one,
For me, and you forever will be.
And I love you so for always.

Come with me my sweet;
Let's go make a family.
And they will bring us joy for always.

Oh boy. I love you so;
I can't find enough ways to let you know.
But you can be sure I'm yours for always.

Always.
Ooh, ooh hoo.
I will love you so for always.

Words & Music by Jonathan Lewis, David Lewis, and Wayne Lewis

Amazed

Ev'ry time our eyes meet,
This feeling inside me
Is almost more than I can take.
Baby, when you touch me,
I can feel how much you love me,
And it just blows me away.
I've never been this close to anyone or anything,
I can hear your thoughts,
I can see your dreams...

Chorus:
I don't know how you do what you do.
I'm so in love with you.
It just keeps getting better.
I wanna spend the rest of my life
With you by my side
Forever and ever.
Ev'ry little thing that you do
Baby, I'm amazed by you.

The smell of your skin,
The taste of your kiss,
The way you whisper in the dark.
Your hair all around me,
Baby, you surround me;
You touch every place in my heart.
Oh, it feels like the first time every time.
I wanna spend the whole night in your eyes.

(Chorus)

Words & Music by Marv Green, Aimee Mayo and Chris Lindsey

AND I LOVE YOU SO

And I love you so.
The people ask me how,
How I've lived till now.
I tell them I don't know.

I guess they understand.
How lonely life has been.
But life began again
The day you took my hand.

And yes I know how lonely life can be
The shadows follow me and the night won't set me free
But I don't let the evening get me down
Now that you're around me

And you love me, too
Your thoughts are just for me;
You set my spirit free.
I'm happy that you do.

The book of life is brief.
And once a page is read
All but love is dead.
That is my belief.

Words & Music By Don McLean

Baby, I Love Your Way

Shadows grow so long before my eyes
And they're moving across the page
Suddenly the day turns into night
Far away from the city
Well, don't hesitate, 'cause your love won't wait...

Chorus:
Ooo, baby, I love your way, everyday
Gonna tell you I love your way, everyday
Wanna be with you night and day

Moon appears to shine and light the skies
With the help of some firefly
Wonder how they have the power to shine
I can see them under the pine
But don't hesitate, 'cause your love won't wait...

(Chorus)

But don't hesitate, 'cause your love won't wait...

I can see the sunset in your eyes
Brown and grey, blue besides
Clouds are stalking islands in the sun
Wish I could buy one out of season
But don't hesitate, 'cause your love won't wait...

(Chorus 2x)

Words & Music by Peter Frampton

Because You Loved Me

For all those times you stood by me
For all the truth that you made me see
For all the joy you brought to my life
For all the wrong that you made right
For every dream you made come true
For all the love I found in you I'll be forever thankful baby
You're the one who held me up - Never let me fall
You're the one who saw me through through it all

Chorus:
You were my strength when I was weak
You were my voice when I couldn't speak
You were my eyes when I couldn't see
You saw the best there was in me
Lifted me up when I couldn't reach
You gave me faith 'coz you believed
I'm everything I am, because you loved me

You gave me wings and made me fly
You touched my hand I could touch the sky
I lost my faith, you gave it back to me
You said no star was out of reach
You stood by me and I stood tall
I had your love I had it all
I'm grateful for each day you gave me
Maybe I don't know that much
But I know this much is true
I was blessed because I was loved by you

(Chorus)

You were always there for me
The tender wind that carried me
A light in the dark shining your love into my life
You've been my inspiration
Through the lies you were the truth
My world is a better place because of you

(Chorus)

I'm everything I am
Because you loved me

Words & Music By Diane Warren

Best Thing That Ever Happened To Me

I've had my share
Of life's ups and downs
But fate's been kind,
The downs have been few

I guess you could say
That I've been lucky
Oh, I guess you could say
That it's all because of you

If anyone should ever write my life story
For whatever reason there might be
Oooh, you'll be there between each line of pain and glory
'Cause you're the best thing
That ever happened to me.
Ah...you're the best thing

Oh...there have been times
When times were hard
But always somehow I made
I made it through

'Cause for every moment
That I've spent hurrying
There was a moment
That I've spent on just loving you, yeah...

If anyone should ever write my life story
For whatever reason,
For whatever reason there might be
Oh...you'll be there between each line of pain and glory
'Cause you're the best thing
Oh, you're the best thing
I know you're the best thing, oh, that ever happened to me.
Hey, hey, hey...

Words & Music by Jim Weatherly

CAN I STEAL
A LITTLE LOVE

Can I steal a little love?
Can I steal a little love?
Coo me, honey, I'm on fire,
To steal your love is my desire.

Hug me, squeeze me, 'till I'm red.
'Til my eyes bug out my head
Coo me, woo me, turtle dove
Can I steal a little love?

Tell me, why are you driving me crazy?
And why do I dig you like I do?
If I should steal a little kiss –
And you can prove that it's wrong
I'll give it back to you

Tell me, honey, with a smile
I can walk you down the isle
I won't even need a shove
Can I steal a little love?

Words & Music by Phil Tuminello

Can't Help Lovin' Dat Man

Chorus:
Fish got to swim, birds got to fly,
I got to love one man till I die.
Can't help lovin' dat man of mine.
Tell me he's lazy, tell me he's slow,
Tell me I'm crazy, (maybe I know).
Can't help lovin' dat man of mine.

Oh listen sister,I love my mister man,
And I can't tell you why
Dere ain't no reason, why I should love dat man,
It mus' be sumpin dat de angels done plan.

(Chorus)

When he goes away, dat's a rainy day,
And when he comes back dat day is fine,
De sun will shine!
He kin come home as late as can be,
Home without him ain't no home to me,
Can't help lovin' dat man of mine.

De chimney's smokin', de roof is leakin' in,
But he don't seem to care.
Dere ain't no reason why I should love dat man.
And why do you love that man?
It mus' be sumpin' dat de angels done plan.

(Chorus)

When he goes away, dat's a rainy day,
And when he comes back, dat day is fine,
De sun will shine!

Yes, sister
He kin come home as late as can be,
Home without him Ain't no home to me,
Can't help lovin'
Dat man of mine.

Words & Music by Oscar Hammerstein II and Jerome Kern

Can't Smile Without You

I can't smile without you.
I can't laugh and I can't walk,
Finding it hard even to talk.

Chorus:
And I feel sad when you're sad.
I feel glad when you're glad.
And you must know what I'm going through,
I just can't smile without you.

You came along just like a song;
You brightened my days.
Who'd believe you were part of a dream
That always seemed light years away?

And you know I can't smile without you.
I can't smile without you.
And you must know what I'm going through,
I just can't smile without you.

Some people say
The happiness way
Is something that hard to find.
Into the new, leaving the old behind me.

(Chorus)

Into the new, leaving the old behind me.

(Chorus)

Words & Music by Chris Arnold, David Martin and Geoff Morrow

Completely

Completely
Wanna give my love, completely.
I'd rather be alone than be in love just half the way.
I want to find someone that I can trust completely,
Wanna give my heart completely
To someone who'll completely give their heart only to me,
And when I find that one, that's when I'll fall in love.

Completely,
Not half, but whole, with heart and soul.

Completely,
Not in between, but everything.

Completely,
That's the way it's got to be,

The way I want someone to fall in love with me,
The way I want someone to fall in love with me.

Words & Music by Diane Warren

DEARLY BELOVED

Chorus:
Dearly beloved, how clearly I see,
Somewhere in heaven you were fashioned for me.
Angel's eyes…knew you,
Angel voices led me to you.

Nothing can stop me…
Fate gave me a sign.
I know that I'll be yours, come shower or shine,
So I say, Clearly,
Dearly beloved, be mine.

(Chorus)

Tell me that it's true,
Tell me you agree,
It was meant for you,
You were meant for me.

Words & Music by Jerome Kern and Johnny Mercer

DEDICATED TO THE ONE I LOVE

While I'm far away from you, my baby,
I know it's hard for you, my baby,
Because, it's hard for me, my baby
And the darkest hour is just before dawn.

Each night before you go to bed, my baby,
Whisper a little prayer for me, my baby,
And tell all the stars above:
This is dedicated to the one I love
(love can never be exactly like we want it to be)

I could be satisfied knowing you love me.
And there's one thing I want you to do especially for me
And it's something that everybody needs

While I'm far away from you, my baby,
I know it's hard for you, my baby,
Because, it's hard for me, my baby
And the darkest hour is just before dawn.

If there's one thing I want you to do especially for me then...

Each night before you go to bed, my baby,
Whisper a little prayer for me, my baby,
And tell all the stars above:
This is dedicated to the one I love
(love can never be exactly like we want it to be)

Words & Music by Lowman Pauling and Ralph Bass

Doin' It
(All For My Baby)

Early in the morning I'm still in bed
She comes to me with sweet affection
Wakes me with kisses, hello sleepyhead
And she gets me moving in the right direction

I do my best to give her love that lasts forever
It seems that everything I do I'm doing better

Doin' it all for my baby
Cause she's as fine as she can be
I'm doin' it all for my baby
For everything she does for me

Then in the evening, it's been a busy day
She lays her head upon my weary shoulder
Listen to her laughing, snuggle up and say
Now I'm with you baby, loneliness is over

I do my best to give her love that lasts forever
It seems that everything I do I'm doing better

Givin' it all for my baby
'Cause she's as fine as she can be
I'm doin' it all for my baby
For everything she does for me

Words & Music by Mike Duke and Phil Cody

Dream Weaver

I just closed my eyes again
Climbed aboard the dream weaver train
Driver, take away my worries of today,
Leave tomorrow behind

Oo Ooh Dream Weaver,
I believe you can get me through the night
Oo Ooh Dream Weaver,
I believe we can reach the morning light

Fly me high through the starry skies,
Or maybe to an astral plane
Cross the highways of fantasy,
Help me to forget today's pain

Oo Ooh Dream Weaver,
I believe you can get me through the night
Oo Ooh Dream Weaver,
I believe we can reach the morning light

Though the dawn may be coming soon,
There still may be some time
Fly me away to the bright side of the moon,
Meet me on the other side

Oo Ooh Dream Weaver,
I believe you can get me through the night
Oo Ooh Dream Weaver,
I believe we can reach the morning light

Words & Music by Gary Wright

Dreaming My Dreams With You

I hope it won't be that wrong anymore
Maybe I've learned this time
I hope that I find what I'm reachin' for
The way it is in my mind

Someday I'll get over you
I'll live to see it all through
But I'll always miss dreaming my dreams with you.

But I won't let it change me, not if I can
I'd rather believe in love
And give it away as much as I can
To those that I'm fondest of.

Someday I'll get over you
I'll live to see it all through
But I'll always miss dreaming my dreams with you.

Someday I'll get over you
I'll live to see it all through
But I'll always miss dreaming my dreams with you

Words & Music by Allen Reynolds

Ebb Tide

First the tide rushes in
Plants a kiss on the shore
Then rolls out to sea
And the sea is very still once more

So I rush to your side
Like the oncoming tide
With one burning thought
Will your arms open wide

At last we're face to face
And as we kiss through an embrace
I can tell, I can feel
You are love, your are real
Really mine in the rain
In the dark, in the sun

Like the tide at its ebb
I'm at peace in the web of your arms

Words by Carl Sigman, Music by Robert Maxwell

ENDLESS LOVE

My love,
There's only you in my life,
The only thing that's right.
My first love,
You're ev'ry breath that I take,
You're ev'ry step I make.
And I, I want to share all my love with you,
No one else will do.
And your eyes,
They tell me how much you care
Oh, yes, you will always be,
My endless love.

Two hearts,
Two hearts that beat as one;
Our lives have just begun.
Forever,
I'll hold you close in my arms,
I can't resist your charms.
And love, I'll be a fool for you I'm sure;
You know I don't mind.
'Cause you,
You mean the world to me.
Oh, I know I've found in you
My endless love.

And yes you'll be the only one
Oh, no, I can't deny this love
I have inside and I'll give it all to you my love,
My endless love.

Words & Music by Lionel Richie

(Everything I Do)
I Do It For You

Look into my eyes, you will see
What you mean to me
Search your heart, search your soul
And when you find me there, you'll search no more

Chorus:
Don't tell me it's not worth tryin' for
You can't tell me it's not worth dyin' for
You know it's true
Everything I do, I do it for you

Look into your heart, you will find
There's nothing there to hide
Take me as I am, take my life
I would give it all, I would sacrifice

(Chorus)

There's no love like your love
And no other could give more love
There's nowhere unless you're there
All the time, all the way, yeah

Oh, you can't tell me it's not worth tryin' for
I can't help it, there's nothin' I want more
Yeah, I would fight for you, I'd lie for you
Walk the wire for you, yeah, I'd die for you

You know it's true
Everything I do
Oooh, I do it for you

Words & Music by Bryan Adams, RJ Lange, and M. Kamen

Everything I Have Is Yours

Ev'rything I have is yours;
You're party of me.
Ev'rything I have is yours, my destiny.

I would gladly give the sun to you
If the sun were only mine.
I would gladly give the earth to you
And the stars that shine.
Ev'rything that I possess I offer you.

Let my dreams of happiness come true.
I'd be happy just to spend my whole life
Waiting at your beck and call.
Ev'rything I have is yours,
My life, my all.

Words & Music by Harold Adamson and Burton Lane

For All We Know

Love, look at the two of us
Strangers in many ways
We've got a lifetime to share
So much to say
And as we go
From day to day
I'll feel you close to me
But time alone will tell
Let's take a lifetime to say
"I knew you well"
For only time will tell us so
And love may grow
For all we know.

Love, look at the two of us
Strangers in many ways
Let's take a lifetime to say
"I knew you well"
For only time will tell us so
And love may grow
For all we know.

Words & Music by
Fred Karlin, James Arthur Griffin, Robb W. Royer.

FOR YOU I WILL

When you're feeling lost in the night,
When you feel your world just ain't right, call on me.
I will be waiting.
Count on me, I will be there.
Anytime the times get too tough,
Anytime your best ain't enough,
I'll be the one to make it better.
I'll be there to protect you, see you through.
I'll be there, and there's nothing I won't do.
I will cross the ocean for you,
I will go and bring you the moon,
I will be your hero, your strength, anything you need.
I will be the sun in your sky,
I will light your way for all time, promise you, therefore I will.

For you I will lay my life on the line.
For you, I'll fight, for you I will die.
With ev'ry breath, with all my soul,
I give you my word, I'll give it all.
Put your faith in me, I'll do anything.

I will shield your heart from the rain,
I won't let no harm come your way.
Oh, these arms will be your shelter,
No, these arms won't let you down.
If there is a mountain to move,
I will move that mountain for you.
I'm here for you, I'm here forever.
I will be a fortress, tall and strong.
I'll keep you safe, I'll stand beside you,
Right or wrong.

Words & Music by Diane Warren

FROM THIS MOMENT ON

From this moment, life has begun.
From this moment, you are the one.
Right beside you is where I belong,
From this moment on.

I give my hand to you with all my heart,
Can't wait to live my life with you, can't wait to start.
You and I will never be apart.
My dreams came true because of you.

From this moment, I have been blessed.
I live only for your happiness,
And for your love I'd give my last breath,
From this moment on.

From this moment, as long as I love,
I will love you, I promise you this.
There is nothing I wouldn't give,
From this moment on.

You're the reason I believe in love.
And you're the answer to my prayers from up above.
All we need is just the two of us.
My dreams came true
Because of you.

Words & Music by Shania Twain and RJ Lange

(God Must Have Spent)
A LITTLE MORE
TIME ON YOU

Can this be true, tell me can this be real?
How can I put into words what I feel?
My life was complete, I thought I was whole;
Why do I feel like I'm losing control?

I never thought that love could feel like this,
Then you changed my world with just one kiss.
How can it be that right here with me,
There's an angel, it's a miracle.

Your love is like a river,
Peaceful and deep.
Your soul is like a secret, that I never could keep.
When I look into your eyes, I know that it's true.
God must have spent a little more time on you.
Oh, a little more time, yes he did, baby.

In all of creation, all things great and small,
You are the one that surpasses them all.
More precious than a diamond or pearl,
They broke the mold when you came in this world.
And I'm trying hard to figure out
Just how I ever did without
The warmth of your smile,
The heart of a child
That's deep inside and leaves me purified.

Your love is like a river,
Peaceful and deep.
Your soul is like a secret that I never could keep.
When I look into your eyes, I know that it's true,
God must have spent a little more time on you.

I never thought that love could feel like this,
Then you changed my world with just one kiss.
How can it be that right here with me,
There's an angel, it's a miracle.

Words & Music by Carl Sturken and Evan Rogers

Have You Ever Really Loved A Woman

To really love a woman, to understand her
You gotta know her deep inside
Hear every thought - see every dream
N' give her wings - when she wants to fly
Then when you find yourself lyin' helpless in her arms
Ya know ya really love a woman

Chorus:
When you love a woman you tell her that she's really wanted
When you love a woman you tell her that she's the one
Cuz she needs somebody to tell her that it's gonna last forever
So tell me have you ever really, really, really ever loved a woman?

To really love a woman
Let her hold you
til ya know how she needs to be touched
You've gotta breathe her - really taste her
Til you can feel her in your blood
N' when you can see
your unborn children in her eyes
Ya know ya really love a woman

(Chorus)

You got to give her some faith - hold her tight
A little tenderness - gotta treat her right
She will be there for you, takin' good care of you
Ya really gotta love your woman...

And when you find yourself lying helpless in her arms,
You know you really love a woman.

(Chorus)

So tell me have you ever really ...
really, really ever loved a woman?

So tell me have you ever really ...
really, really ever loved a woman?

Words & Music by Bryan Adams, RJ Lange and M. Kamen

Heaven

Oh, thinkin' about all our younger years
There was only you and me
We were young and wild and free
Now nothin' can take you away from me
We've been down that road before
But that's over now
You keep me comin' back for more

Chorus:
Baby you're all that I want
When you're lyin' here in my arms
I'm findin' it hard to believe
We're in heaven
And love is all that I need
And I found it there in your heart
It isn't too hard to see
We're in heaven

Oh, once in your life you find someone
Who will turn your world around
Bring you up when you're feelin' down
Yeah, nothin' could change what you mean to me
Oh, there's lots that I could say
But just hold me now
'Cause our love will light the way

(Chorus)

I've been waitin' for so long
For somethin' to arrive
For love to come along
Now our dreams are comin' true
Through the good times and the bad
Yeah, I'll be standin' there by you

(Chorus)

Words & Music by Bryan Adams and Jim Vallance

HEAVEN MUST BE MISSING AN ANGEL

Heaven must be missin' an angel
Missin' one angel, child, 'cause you're here with me right now
Your love is heavenly, baby
Heavenly to me, baby

Your kiss with tenderness
I want all I can get of your sexiness
Showers, your love comes in showers
And every hour of the hour
You let me feel your loving power

There's a rainbow over my shoulder [Ooh, ooh]
When you came, my cup runneth over
You gave me your heavenly love
And if one night you hear crying from above

Ooh...I'm captured by your spell [Ooh, ooh]
You're different, girl, I can tell [Ooh...ooh...ooh...]
When you're layin' on my pillow, baby
Above your pretty head, there's a halo, that's why I know

You must have slipped away along the Milky Way
It's 'cause [Your kiss] your kiss [Filled with tenderness]
You came C.O.D. on a moonbeam straight to me
Just like [Showers, showers, showers, showers] showers
[Showers, showers, showers]

Your heavenly power gets stronger by the hour
Heaven must be missin' an angel
I'm captured by your spell, oh, girl, can't you tell
Heaven (Heaven) must be missin' an angel

Words & Music by K. St. Lewis and Freddie Perren

HOLD ME
(In Your Arms)

I hold you, I touch you
Make you my woman, I'll give you my love
With sweet surrender, Tonight our hearts will beat as one
And I'll hold you, I'll touch you
Make you my woman tonight

There's something in your eyes I see
A pure and simple honesty

Chorus:
Hold me in your arms tonight, fill my life with pleasure
Let's not waste this precious time, this moment's ours to treasure
Hold me in your arms tonight
We'll make it last forever
When the morning sun appears
We'll find our way together

I believe you
When you say that you love me
Know that I won't take you for granted
Tonight the magic has begun
So won't you hold me touch me
Make me a woman tonight

There's something in your eyes I see
I won't betray your trust in me

(Chorus)

I'll hold you (hold)
And touch you (Touch me baby)
Make you my woman (Make me a woman)
Tonight

Words & Music by Michael Masser and Linda Creed

I Believe In You And Me

I believe in you and me,
I believe that we will be
In love eternally.
Well, as far as I can see,
You will always be the one for me.
Oh yes, you will.
I believe in dreams again,
I believe that love will never end,
And like the river finds the sea,

I was lost, now I'm free,
'Cause I believe in you and me.

I will never leave your side,
I will never hurt your pride.
When all the chips are down,
I will always be around,
Just to be right where you are, my love.
Oh, I love you, boy,
I will never leave you out,
I will always let you in to places no one has ever been.
Deep inside, can't you see?
I believe in you and me.

Maybe I'm a fool to feel the way I do,
But I would play the fool forever
Just to be with you forever.
I believe in miracles,
And love's a miracle,
And yes, baby, you're my dream come true.

I was lost, now I'm free,
'Cause I believe in you and me.
See I'm lost, now I'm free,
'Cause I believe in you and me.

Words & Music by Sandy Linzer and David Wolfert

I Can't Begin To Tell You

I never have a dream
That I don't see you in it.
You never leave my thought,
No, not even for a minute.
And if you should ask me
How deeply I adore you,
I would simply reply:

I can't begin to tell you
How much you mean to me.
My world will end if ever we were through.
I can't begin to tell you
How happy I would be,
If I could speak my mind like others do.
I make such pretty speeches,
Whenever we're apart.
But when you're near,
The words I choose refuse to leave my heart.
So, take the sweetest phrases
The world has ever known,
And make believe I've said them all to you.

Words & Music by Mack Gordon and James V. Monaco

I CROSS MY HEART

Our love is unconditional
We knew it from the start
I can see it in your eyes
You can feel it from my heart
From here on after
Let's stay the way we are right now
And share all the love and laughter
That a lifetime will allow

Chorus:
I cross my heart
And promise to
Give all I've got to give
To make all your dreams come true
In all the world
You'll never find
A love as true as mine

You will always be the miracle
That makes my life complete
And as long as there's still breath in me
I'll make yours just as sweet
As we look into the future
It's as far as we can see
So let's make each tomorrow
Be the best that it can be

(Chorus)

And if along the way we find a day
It starts to pour
You've got the promise of my love
To keep you warm

Words & Music by Steve Dorff and Eric Kaz

I FINALLY FOUND SOMEONE

I finally found someone, that knocks me off my feet
I finally found the one, that makes me feel complete
We started over coffee, we started out as friends
It's funny how from simple things, the best things begin

This time it's different, dah dah dah dah
It's all because of you, dah dah dah dah
It's better than it's ever been
'Cause we can talk it through
Oohh, my favorite line was "Can I call you sometime?"
It's all you had to say to take my breath away

This is it, oh, I finally found someone
Someone to share my life
I finally found the one, to be with every night
'Cause whatever I do, it's just got to be you
My life has just begun
I finally found someone, ooh, someone
I finally found someone, oooh

Did I keep you waiting, I didn't mind
I apologize, baby, that's fine
I would wait forever just to know you were mine
And I love your hair, sure it looks fine
I love what you wear, isn't it the time?
You're exceptional, I can't wait for the rest of my life

This is it, oh, I finally found someone
Someone to share my life
I finally found the one, to be with every night
'Cause whatever I do, it's just got to be you

My life has just begun

Words & Music by Bryan Adams, Barbra Streisand,
Marvin Hamlisch and RJ Lange

I HONESTLY LOVE YOU

Maybe I hang around here
A little more than I should
We both know I got somewhere else to go
But I got something to tell you
That I never thought I would
But I believe you really ought to know

I love you, I honestly love you

You don't have to answer
I see it in your eyes
Maybe it was better left unsaid
This is pure and simple
And you should realize
That it's coming from my heart and not my head

I love you, I honestly love you

I'm not trying to make you feel uncomfortable
I'm not trying to make you anything at all
But this feeling doesn't come along everyday
And you shouldn't blow the chance
When you've got the chance to say

I love you, I honestly love you

If we both were born
In another place and time
This moment might be ending in a kiss
But there you are with yours
And here I am with mine
So I guess we'll just be leaving it at this

I love you
I honestly love you
I honestly love you

Words & Music by Peter Allen and Jeff Barry

(I Love You)
FOR SENTIMENTAL REASONS

Chorus:
I love you for sentimental reasons
I hope you do believe me
I'll give you my heart

I love you
And you alone were meant for me
Please give your loving heart to me
And say we'll never part

I think of you every morning
Dream of you every night
Darling, I'm never lonely
Whenever you're in sight

(Chorus)

I think of you every morning
Dream of you every night
Darling, I'm never lonely
Whenever you're in sight

By Deek Watson & William Best

I Love You
Too Much

I love you much too much
I bear no hatred toward you
I love you much too much
To be angry with you.

I love you much too much
To be really mad at you,
Call me a fool, I know,
But I love you still.

I gave you my life,
My heart, my soul.
Although I'm in pain, my mind
Harbors no thoughts of vengeance....

I love you much too much
To be really angry with you,
Call me a fool, I know,
But I love you still.

Words & Music by Don Raye, Alex Olshanetsky, Chaim Towber.

I Only Have Eyes For You

Are the stars out tonight?
I don't know if it's cloudy or bright,
'Cause I only have eyes for you, dear.
The moon may be high,
But I can't see a thing in the sky,
'Cause I only have eyes for you.

I don't know if we're in a garden,
Or on a crowded avenue.
You are here, so am I,
Maybe millions of people go by,
But they all disappear from view,
And I only have eyes for you.

Words by Al Dubin, Music by Harry Warren

I PLEDGE MY LOVE

I will love you till the day I die
I know this now and my love won't run dry
You came along, my life has begun
Two hearts are now beating as though they were one

Like the stars that make the night so bright
You shine on me with a love that's so right
A love that is lasting, a love that's so pure
Each time I feel it, it makes me more sure

I know with all my heart we'll never part
For this is the day when our love comes alive
And I mean what I say
As I stand here saying

Chorus:
I pledge my love to you
I pledge my love is true
I pledge my life to you
I do, my dear, I do my, dear

Like a river finds the deep blue sea
Love took your hand and led you to me
This is the us that I'll never forget
Both sparkling with love, both happy we met

I know with all my heart we'll never part
For this is the day when our love comes alive
And I mean every word and I want you to know that

(Chorus)

I'm so proud to have you by my side
You'll be my strength and I'll be your guide
You are the one, you're a dream that is real
Heaven has sent you, it's love that I feel
I know with all my heart we'll never part
For this is the day that our love comes alive
And I mean what I say if somebody should ask me

(Chorus)

Words & Music by Dino Fekaris and Freddie Perren

I Swear

I swear
By the moon and the stars in the skies
And I swear
Like the shadow that's by your side

I see the questions in your eyes
I know what's weighing on your mind
You can be sure I know my part

'Cause I stand beside you through the years
You'll only cry those happy tears
And though I make mistakes
I'll never break your heart

Chorus:
And I swear
By the moon and the stars in the skies
I'll be there
I swear
Like the shadow that's by your side
I'll be there
For better or worse
Till death do us part
I'll love you
With every beat of my heart
And I swear
Ooh, ooh, ooh

I'll give you everything I can
I'll build your dreams with these two hands
We'll hang some memories
On the walls

And when (And when) just the two of us are there
You won't have to ask if I still care
'Cause as the time turns the page
My love won't age at all

(Chorus 2x)

Words & Music by Gary Baker and Frank Myers

I WISH YOU LOVE

Goodbye, no use leading with our chins,
This is where our story ends,
Never lovers, ever friends.

Goodbye, let our hearts call it a day,
But before you walk away,
I sincerely want to say –

I wish you bluebirds in the spring
To give your heart a song to sing;
And then a kiss, but more than this,
I wish you love.

And in July a lemonade
To cool you in some leafy glade;
I wish you health, but more than wealth
I wish you love.

My breaking heart and I agree
that you and I could never be;
So with my best, my very best
I set you free.

I wish you shelter from the storm;
A cozy fire to keep you warm,
But most of all when snow flakes fall,
I wish you love.

Words & Music by Albert A. Beach and Charles Trenet

IF I EVER FALL IN LOVE

The very first time
That I saw your brown eyes,
Your lips said hello and I said hi.
I knew right then you were the one,
But I was caught up
In physical attraction.
But to my satisfaction
Baby, you were more than just a face.

And if I ever (ever fall) in love again (again)
I will be sure that the lady is a friend
And if I ever (ever fall) in love so true (true)
I will be sure that the lady's just like you

Oh, yeah, the very next time she'll be my friend

If I say that I will be your one and only
(promise, promise) Promise that you'll never leave me lonely
I just wanna be the one you need
Oh, baby
I just wanna be the one who serves you
Sometime I feel as if I don't deserve you
I cherish every moment that we share

(repeat)

Very next time she will be my friend
Someone who I can believe in
(my friend)
I need someone who'll be my friend
(my friend)
To be with me through thick and thin
(my friend)
Please share my love with me my friend
I need someone like you

Words & Music by Carl Martin

IF WE HOLD
ON TOGETHER

Don't lose your way, with each passing day
You've come so far, don't throw it away
Live believing - dreams are for weaving
Wonders are waiting to start

Live your story- faith hope and glory
Hold to the truth in your heart

Chorus:
If we hold on together
I know our dreams will never die
Dreams see us through to forever
Where clouds roll by, for you and I

Souls in the wind must learn how to bend
Seek out a star; hold on to the end
Valley, mountain, there is a fountain
Washes our tears all away

Worlds are swaying
Someone is praying
Please let them come home to stay

(Chorus)

When we are out there in the dark
We'll dream about the sun
In the dark we'll feel the light
Warm our hearts everyone

(Chorus)

Words & Music by James Horner and Will Jennings

If You Asked Me To

Used to be that I believed in something,
Used to be that I believed in love.
It's been a long time since I've had that feeling:
I could love someone, I could trust someone.
I said I'd never let nobody near my heart again, darlin',
I said I'd never let nobody in.

But if you asked me to,
I just might change my mind
And let you in my life forever.
If you asked me to,
I just might give my heart
And stay here in your arms forever.
If you asked me to.

Somehow ever since I've been around you,
Can't go back to being on my own.
Can't help feeling, darling, since I've found you
That I've found my home.
That I'm finally home.

I said I'd never let nobody get too close to me, darlin',
I said I needed, needed to be free.
But ask me to I will give you world to you, baby.
I need you now.
Ask me to.
I'll do anything for you, baby, for you, baby,
If you asked me to.

Words & Music by Diane Warren

IF YOU SAY MY
EYES ARE BEAUTIFUL

Chorus:
If you say my eyes are beautiful,
It's because they're looking at you.
And if you could only see yourself
You'd feel the same way too.
You could say that I am a dreamer
Who's had a dream come true.
If you say my eyes are beautiful,
It's because they're looking at you.

If you wonder why I'm smiling,
It's because I'm happy with you,
And the warm sensations touch my heart
And fill me through and through.
I could hold you close forever
And never let you go.
If you say my eyes are beautiful,
It's because I just love you so.
Oh.
Now my heart is an open door.
Won't you come inside for more?
You give love so sweetly now.
Take my love,
Take me completely now.
Oh.

(Chorus)

Words & Music by Elliot Willensky

LADY

Chorus:
You're my lady
You're my lady
You're my lady
You're my lady

Don't think I don't see them looking at ya
All of them wishing they could have ya
And as a matter of fact, uh
A bunch of them are itchin' for you to scratch 'em
I'm tired of hiding what we feel
I'm trying to come with the real
And I'm-a gonna make it known, cause I want them to know

(Chorus)

You're my little baby, my darling baby
I swear you're the talk of the town
And everybody wants to know what's going down
Babe, I know they've seen us before
Maybe at the liquor store, or maybe at the health food stand
They don't know that I'm your man

(Chorus)

I can tell they're looking at us
I pick you up everyday from your job
And every guy in the parking lot wants to rob me of my girl
And my heart and soul, and everybody wants to treat me so cold
But I know I love you and you love me
There's no other lover for you or me
You're my lady
You're my lady
My divine lady
You're my lady
Such a wonderful lady
I can tell they're looking at us

Words & Music by Michael Archer and Rafael Saadiq

Long Ago
(And Far Away)

Long ago and far away,
I dreamed a dream one day,
And now that dream is here beside me!

Long the skies were overcast,
But now the clouds have past,
You're here at last!

Chills run up and down my spine,
Aladdin's lamp is mine,
The dream I dreamed was not denied me!

Just one look and then I knew,
That all I longed for long ago,
Was you!

Long ago, so long ago and far away!
So long ago!
So long ago and far away,
I dreamed a dream one-day,
And now that dream is here beside me!
Long the skies were overcast,
But now the clouds have past,
You're here at last!

Chills run up and down my spine,
Aladdin's lamp is mine,
The dream I dreamed was not denied me!

Just one look and then I knew,
That all I longed for long ago,
So long ago, was you!

Words & Music by Jerome Kern and Ira Gershwin

LOOK HEART, NO HANDS

I remember how it used to feel
Riding down old two mile hill
Tennis shoes up on the handle bars
Paying no mind to the passing cars
No doubts, no fears, just like when you are here

Chorus:
No chains, no strings, no fences, no wall
No net, just you to catch me when I fall
Look heart, no hands.
It took a little time to get up to speed
To find the confidence and strength I need
To just let go and reach for the sky
You know sometimes it felt I could fly.
No doubts, no fears, just like when you are here.

(Chorus)

It doesn't take much, just a smile or a touch
And I'm a kid again, I can almost feel that wind
Look heart, no hands, then play full chord to end

Words & Music by Howard Smith and Trey Bruce

L-O-V-E

I started to write this song about you
And then I decided that I would write it all about love

And it appeared to me
That you wasn't happy
And that's for sure, positively
That's what the world is made of
So give me more L-O-V-E, love
Love is a walk down Main Street (oh love)
Love is an apple that is so sweet (oh love)
Love is something that can't be beat (love)

L-O-V-E is strange to me, Oh
I can't explain this feeling
Can't you see that salvation is freeing
It's all in the heavens, can't you see
You can always depend on me
To give you love

Love is a flower in my soul (oh love)
Love is a story that just can't be told (love)
Can't you feel it burning more and more (love)

Stop and look at the big wheel roll
I can't explain this feeling
Can't you see that salvation is freeing
I would give my life for the glory
Just to be able to tell the story
About love

I didn't mean to make you mad
A sweet story, I thought I had
But maybe time will bring us together
And I can be such a happy fella
About love

Love is something that is so divine (oh love)
Love is a feeling that's a friend of mine (love)

It can't be measured by no sign (love)
In your heart or even in your mind
About love, Love is as bright as the morning sun

Words & Music by Al Green, Mabon Hodges, Willie Mitchell.

LOVE AND MARRIAGE

Love and marriage, love and marriage
Go together like a horse and carriage
This I tell you brother
You can't have one without the other

Love and marriage, love and marriage
It's an institute you can't disparage
Ask the local gentry
And they will say it's elementary

Try, try, try to separate them
It's an illusion
Try, try, try, and you will only come
To this conclusion

Love and marriage, love and marriage
Go together like a horse and carriage
Dad was told by mother
You can't have one without the other

Words & Music by Sammy Cahn and Jimmy Van Heusen

LOVE IS ALIVE

Well I think it's time to get ready
To relax just what I have found
I have lived only half of what I am
All clear to me now

Chorus:
My heart is on fire
My soul's like a wheel that's turnin'
Your love is alive, my love is alive

Three's something inside
That's making me crazy
I'll try to keep it together
'Cause what I say may not happen the same way
Now could be forever

(Chorus)

There's a mirror moving inside my mind
Reflecting the love that you shine on me
Hold on now to that feeling
Let it flow, let it grow

(Repeat Chorus)

Words & Music by Gary Wright

Love Is A Many-Splendored Thing

I walked along the streets of Hong Kong town,
Up and down, up and down.
I met a little girl in Hong Kong town,
And I said, "Can you tell me, please,
Where's that love I've never found?
Unravel me this riddle:
What is love? What can it be?"
And in her eyes were butterflies as she replied to me.

Love is a many-splendored thing,
It's the April rose that only grows in the early Spring;
Love is nature's way of giving
A reason to be living,
The golden crown that makes a man a king.
Once on a high and windy hill,
In the morning mist two lovers kissed
And the world stood still.
Then your fingers touched my silent heart
And taught it how to sing.
Yes, true love's a many-splendored thing.

(Repeat)

Words by Paul Francis Webster, Music by Sammy Fain

LOVE LIKE OURS

I look at you and there it is,
The ultimate in where it is,
And realize how rare it is,
This finding your love.
You try so many arms
When you are lonely,
To find the one and only.
One day you turn and she's (he's) there.
Amazing how serene it is,
The shade of evergreen it is,
Exactly what we mean it is,
And knew it would be.

When love like ours arrives,
We guard it with our lives.
Whatever goes astray,
What rainy day comes around,
A love like ours will keep us safe and sound.

Words by Alan and Marilyn Bergman,
Music by Dave Grusin

LOVE, ME

I read a note my grandma wrote back in nineteen twenty-three.
Grandpa kept it in his coat, and he showed it once to me.
He said, "Boy you might not understand, but a long, long time ago,
Grandma's daddy didn't like me none, but I loved your Grandma so."

We had this crazy plan to meet and run away together.
Get married in the first town we came to and live forever.
But nailed to the tree where we were supposed to meet instead,
I found this letter, and this is what it said:

If you get there before I do,
Don't give up on me.
I'll meet you when my chores are through.
I don't know how long I'll be.
But I'm not gonna let you down.
Darling, wait and see.
And between now and then,
Till I see you again,
I'll be loving you.
Love, me.

I read those words just hours before my Grandma passed away,
In the doorway of a church where me and Grandpa stopped to pray.
I know I'd never seen him cry in all my fifteen years;
But as he said these words to her, his eyes filled up with tears.

If you get there before I do,
Don't give up on me.
I'll meet you when my chores are through.
I don't know how long I'll be.
But I'm not gonna let you down.
Darling, wait and see.
And between now and then,
Till I see you again,
I'll be loving you.
Love, me.

And between now and then,

Till I see you again,
I'll be loving you.
Love, me.

Words & Music by Skip Ewing and Max T. Barnes

LOVE WILL FIND A WAY

Someone, someone's got me wrong
You thought that your love was strong
Now you're feelin' like such a fool
Poor you, you're thinkin' maybe if you said goodbye
You'll understand the reason why
The love you had felt so cool, mmm, hmm

Oh, but it's alright
Once you get past the pain
You'll learn to find your love again
So keep your heart open
'Cause love will find a way

Sometimes we all feel a need to change
Our love we have to rearrange
And move on to something new, yes, you do
Your dreams feel like they're fallin' apart
You need to find a brand new start
But you're almost afraid to be true to yourself

Oh, but it's all right
Once you get past the pain
You'll learn to find your love again
So keep your heart open
'Cause love will find a way

Love will find a way
Love will find a way

So now don't, don't be afraid of yourself
Just move on to something else
And let your love shine through
Again yes, 'cause it's all right
Once you get past the pain
You'll learn to find your love again
So keep your heart open
'Cause love will find a way

Words & Music By David Jenkins and Cory Lerios

MAKIN' WHOOPEE!

Another bride, another June,
Another sunny honeymoon;
Another season, another reason
For makin' whoopee!

A lot of shoes, a lot of rice,
The groom is nervous, he answers twice;
It's really killing that he's so willing
To make whoopee!

Picture a little love nest
Down where the roses cling;
Picture the same sweet love nest,
Think what a year can bring.

He's washing dishes and baby clothes,
He's so ambitious, he even sews;
But don't forget, folks,
That's what you get, folks,
For makin' whoopee!

Words by Gus Kahn, Music by Walter Donaldson

Misty

Look at me,
I'm as helpless as a kitten up a tree,
And I feel like I'm clinging to a cloud;
I can't understand,
I get misty just holding your hand.
Walk my way
And a thousand violins begin to play,
Or it might be the sound of your hello,
That music I hear,
I get misty the moment you're near.
You can say that you're leading me on,
But it's just what I want you to do.
Don't you notice how hopelessly I'm lost?
That's why I'm following you.
On my own,
Would I wander through this wonderland alone,
Never knowing my right foot from my left,
My hat from my glove.
I'm too misty and too much in love.

Words by Johnny Burke, Music by Erroll Garner

MORE THAN WORDS

Saying I love you
Is not the words I want to hear from you
It's not that I want you not to say,
But if you only knew
How easy it would be to show me how you feel
More than words is all you have to do
to make it real
Then you wouldn't have to say that you love me

'Cause I'd already know

What would you do if my heart was torn in two?
More than words to show you feel
That your love for me is real
What would you say if I took those words away?
Then you couldn't make things new
Just by saying I love you

More than words.....

Now that I've tried to talk to you and make you understand
All you have to do is close your eyes
And just reach out your hands and touch me
Hold me close don't ever let me go
More than words
is all I ever needed you to show
Then you wouldn't have to say that you love me
'Cause I'd already know

What would you do if my heart was torn in two?
More than words to show you feel
That your love for me is real
What would you say if I took those words away?
Then you couldn't make things new
Just by saying I love you

More than words...

Words & Music by Gary Cherone and Nuno Bettencourt

Now And Forever
(You and Me)

Up until now
I've learned to live without love;
Like a ship without a sail,
Wandering aimlessly lost.
I never knew how it felt
To lose my control,
But now that I've found you, This is all so new.

Chorus:
You and me,
We've got a destiny starting tonight;
We'll be together.
You and me;
This is what love should be,
And it's gonna be right;
Now and forever.

Darlin',
Inside your eyes,
I can see mysteries there.
And you're melting the ice surrounding me;
I'm no longer scared.
I feel you inside my soul.
And I'm captured tonight.
But don't let go; This is paradise.

(Chorus)

If you tell me
There's a heaven up above,
Then that's what I'll believe,
'Cause you're the one thing that I'm so sure of.

I feel you inside my soul,
And I'm captured tonight.
But don't let go;
This is paradise.

(Chorus)

Words & Music by Jim Vallance, David Foster and Randy Goodrum

On the Wings of Love

Just smile for me and let the day begin.
You are the sunshine that lights my heat within.
I'm sure that you're an angel in disguise.
Come take my hand and together we will rise.

Chorus:
On the wings of love,
Up and above the clouds
The only way to fly
Is on the wings of love.
On the wings of love,
Only the two of us
Together flying high.
Flying high upon the wings of love.

You look at me and I begin to melt,
Just like the snow when a ray of sun is felt.
I'm crazy about you baby, can't you see?
I'd be delighted if you could come with me.

(Chorus)

Yes, you belong to me.
I'm yours exclusively.
Right now we live and breathe each other,
Inseparable it seems,
We're flowing like a stream,
Running free flowing
On the wings of love.

(Chorus)

Words & Music by
Jeffrey Osborne and Peter Harrison Schless

ONE IN A MILLION YOU

Love had played its game on me so long.
I started to believe I'd never find anyone.
Doubt had tried to convince me to give in,
Said you can't win.

But one day the sun it came a shinin' through.
The rain had stopped, and the skies were blue.
And oh, what a revelation to see.
Someone was saying "I love you " to me.

Chorus:
A one in a million, chance of a lifetime.
And life showed compassion.
And sent to me a stroke of love called you.
A one in a million you.

I was a lonely man with empty arms to fill.
Then I found a piece of happiness to call my own.
And life is worth living again.
For to love you to me is to live.

(Chorus 2x)

Words & Music by Sam Dees

Remember What I Told You To Forget

Hello baby
I betcha never thought I would call
Well my heart just went in with this dime
And I only get three minutes time
Hear me out now
I wanna to make it as clear as I can
There's so much that I want to explain
And the final decision remains
In you hands

Please remember what I told you to forget
There's a man on the phone
And he wants to come home
To the woman he loves all alone

Baby remember what I told you to forget
No I won't waste anytime when I hang up the line
I'll be back in your arms
Where I know I belong

One more minute
Let me pour my heart out to you
'Cause I've kept it all locked up inside
You just can't tell your own foolish pride what to do

So remember what I told you to forget
No I wouldn't waste anytime when I hang up the line
I'll be back in your arms
Where I know I belong

If it isn't already too late
Let me give you a reason to wait
For the life that I'm begging to live
Will depend on the answer you give

Please remember what I told you to forget
There's a man on the phone
And he wants to come home
To the woman he loves all alone

Words & Music by Dennis Lambert and Brian Potter

SACRED EMOTION

There's a candle I keep in my window,
and it's burning brighter tonight.
Through the storm and the winds of change,
I'll be sure that you can see the light.
I never wandered, I never gave up,
'cause a true heart never goes astray.
Whatever road that you take
will lead you back to me,
'cause our love is too strong to slip away.

Chorus:
Like a river flowing into the ocean,
I can feel you coming back to me.
(bring it on back)
'Cause our love is like a sacred emotion,
and it's burning bright
for the whole world to see.

It won't be long before I hear
that knock on my door, that telephone call.
And if your journey takes you far away,
I'll still catch you when you fall.
Love's like a wheel, turning 'round and round,
the feeling fades but never dies.
There'll never be any question
or doubt in my mind,
'cause the answer's right there, in your eyes.

(Chorus)

Whatever road that you take
will lead you back to me
'cause our love is too strong to slip away.
Like a river flowing into the ocean,
(bring it on back to me)
I can feel you coming back to me.
(I feel you in my heart)

Words & Music by Carl Sturken and Evan Rogers

She Believes In Me

While she lays sleeping, I stay out late at night and play my songs
And sometimes all the nights can be so long
And it's good when I finally make it home, all alone
While she lays dreaming, I try to get undressed without the light
And quietly she says how was your night?
And I come to her and say, it was all right, and I hold her tight

Chorus:
And she believes in me, I'll never know just what she sees in me
I told her someday if she was my girl, I could change the world
With my little songs, I was wrong
But she has faith in me, and so I go on trying faithfully
And who knows maybe on some special night, if my song is right
I will find a way, find a way...

While she lays waiting, I stumble to the kitchen for a bite
Then I see my old guitar in the night
Just waiting for me like a secret friend, and there's no end
While she lays crying, I fumble with a melody or two
And I'm torn between the things that I should do
And she says to wake her up when I am through,
God her love is true.

Words & Music by Steve Gibb

SHE IS HIS ONLY NEED

Billy was a small town loner who never did dream
Of ever leaving southern Arizona
Or ever hearing wedding bells ring
He never had a lot of luck with the ladies
But he sure had a lot of good working skills
Never cared about climbing any ladder
He knew the way in a small cafe, found the will

He met Miss Bonnie and a little bit of her was a little too much
A few movies and a few months later the feeling got strong enough
They didn't own a car, so it must have been love
That drove him uptown for a diamond - that's when he started goin'

Over the line, working overtime

To give her things just to hear her say she don't deserve them
But he loves her and he just kept going overboard
Over the limit to afford to give her things he knew she wanted
'Cause without her where would he be?

See, it's not for him, she is his only need

Ring on her finger and one on the ladder
A new promotion every now and then

Bonnie worked until she couldn't tie her apron
Then stayed at home and had the first of two children
And my, how the time did fly.
The babies grew up and moved away left 'em sitting on the front porch rocking
And Billy watching Bonnie's hair turn gray

And ev'ry once in a while you could see him get up
And he'd head downtown, cause he heard about something she wanted
And it just had to be found. Didn't matter how simple or how much
It was love , and, boy, ain't that love just something
When it's strong enough to keep a man goin'

Over the line, working overtime
She is his only need, his only need

Overboard, over the limit, just for her
She is his only need, his only need

Words & Music by David Loggins

SHINING STAR

You are my shining star. Don't you go away.
Wanna be right here where you are until my dying day.

So many have tried, tried to find a love like yours and mine
Girl, don't your realize how you hypnotize?

Make me, love you more each time.
Honey I'll never leave you lonely;
give my love to you only, to you only, to you only.

Honey, you are my shining star. Don't you go away.
Wanna be right here where you are until my dying day.

Feels so good when we're lying here next to each other, lost in love.
Baby, when we touch, love you so much.
You're all I ever dreamed of.

Honey I'll never leave you lonely;
give my love to you only, to you only, to you only.

Honey, you are my shining star. Don't you go away.
Wanna be right here where you are until my dying day.

Words & Music by Leo Graham and Paul Richmond

Smoke Gets In Your Eyes

They asked me how I knew my true love was true
I of course replied "something here inside cannot be denied"
They said "someday you'll find all who love are blind"
When your heart's on fire, you must realize smoke gets in your eyes
So I chaffed them and I gaily laughed to think they could doubt my love
Yet today my love has flown away, I am without my love

Now laughing friends deride tears I cannot hide
So I smile and say "when a lovely flame dies, smoke gets in your eyes"
Smoke gets in your eyes
Smoke gets in your eyes
Smoke-gets-in-your-EYES

Words by Otto Harbach, Music by Jerome Kern

SOMEWHERE OUT THERE

Somewhere out there
Beneath the pale moonlight
Someone's thinking of me
And loving me tonight

Somewhere out there
Someone's saying a prayer
That we'll find one another
In that big somewhere out there

And even though I know
How very far apart we are
It helps to think we might be wishing
On the same bright star

And when the night wind
Starts to sing a lonesome lullaby
It helps to think we're sleeping
Underneath the same big sky

Somewhere out there
If love can see us through
Then we'll be together
Somewhere out there
Out where dreams come true

And even though I know
How very far apart we are
It helps to think we might be wishing
on the same bright star

And when the night wind
Starts to sing a lonesome lullaby
It helps to think we're sleeping
Underneath the same big sky

Somewhere out there
If love can see us through
Then we'll be together
Somewhere out there
Out where dreams come true...

Words & Music by James Horner, Barry Mann and Cynthia Weil

STAND BY YOUR MAN

Sometimes it's hard to be a woman,
Giving your love to just one man.
You'll have bad times,
He'll have good times,
Doing things that you don't understand.

But if you love him you'll forgive him,
Even though he's hard to understand.
If you love him,
Be proud of him,
'Cause after all he's just a man.

Stand by your man,
Give him two arms to cling to
And something warm to come to
When the nights are cold and lonely.

Stand by your man
And tell the world you love him,
Keep giving all the love you can.
Stand by your man.

Stand by your man
And show the world you love him,
Keep giving all the love you can.
Stand by your man.

Words & Music by Tammy Wynette and Billy Sherrill

SUNRISE, SUNSET

Is this the little girl I carried?
Is this the little boy at play?
I don't remember growing older.
When did they?
When did she get to be a beauty?
When did he grow to be so tall?
Wasn't it yesterday when they were small?

Chorus:
Sunrise, Sunset,
Sunrise, Sunset,
Swiftly flow the days.
Seedlings turn overnight to sunflowers,
Blossoming even as we gaze.
Sunrise, Sunset,
Sunrise, Sunset,
Swiftly fly the years.
One season following another,
Laden with happiness and tears.

What words of wisdom can I give them?
How can I help to ease their way?
Now they must learn from one another,
Day by day.
They look so natural together,
Just like two newlyweds should be.
Is there a canopy in store for me?

(Chorus)

Lyrics by Sheldon Harnick, Music by Jerry Bock

Sweet Nothin's

My baby whispers in my ear
mmm, Sweet Nothin's
He knows the things I like to hear
mmm, Sweet Nothin's

Things he wouldn't tell nobody else
Secret baby, I keep them to myself
mmm, mmm, Sweet Nothin's

We walk along hand in hand
mmm, Sweet Nothin's
Yeah we both understand
mmm, Sweet Nothin's

Sittin' in classroom trying to read my book
My baby Sweet Nothin's gives me that special look
mmm, mmm, Sweet Nothin's

Ah sittin' on my front porch
mmm, Sweet Nothin's
Well do I love you, of course
mmm, Sweet Nothin's

Mama turned on the front porch light
Sayin' "Come here darlin' that' enough for tonight"
mmm, mmm, Sweet Nothin's
mmm, mmm, Sweet Nothin's

Words & Music by Ronnie Self

THE BEST YEARS OF MY LIFE

Ev'ry time I feel
How life goes by
I recall the scenes that never die
One fine day
One fine night
You loving me on and on
We took our love as far as love can go

Ohh, ohh,
You've given me the best years of my life
The best years of my life

Bring on the storm
We'll see it through
We'll take it all, all life can do.
Right to the end,
We'll say "Let's Begin."

You've given me the best years of my life
I want to thank you
I want to thank you
You've given me the best years of me life

When I play my memories again.
I feel all the pleasure and the pain
Love can hurt, love can heal
Oh, how we hurt and heal ourselves again.

We took our souls as far as souls can go, ooh yeah.
You've given me the best years of my life
You've given me the best years of my life.

Words & Music by Will Jennings and Stephen Allen Davis

THE GREATEST LOVE OF ALL

I believe the children are our are future
Teach them well and let them lead the way
Show them all the beauty they possess inside
Give them a sense of pride to make it easier
Let the children's laughter remind us how we used to be

Everybody searching for a hero
People need someone to look up to
I never found anyone who fulfill my needs
A lonely place to be
So I learned to depend on me

Chorus:
I decided long ago, never to walk in anyone's shadows
If I fail, if I succeed
At least I'll live as I believe
No matter what they take from me
They can't take away my dignity
Because the greatest love of all
Is happening to me
I found the greatest love of all
Inside of me
The greatest love of all
Is easy to achieve
Learning to love yourself
It is the greatest love of all

I believe the children are our future
Teach them well and let them lead the way
Show them all the beauty they possess inside
Give them a sense of pride to make it easier
Let the children's laughter remind us how we used to be

(Chorus)

And if by chance, that special place
That you've been dreaming of
Leads you to a lonely place
Find your strength in love

Words & Music by Michael Masser and Linda Creed

The More
I See You

Each time I look at you,
It's like the first time.
Each time you're near me,
The thrill is new.
And there is nothing that I wouldn't do for
The rare delight of
The sight of you.
For...

The more I see you,
The more I want you.
Somehow this feeling
Just grows and grows.
With every sigh,
I become more mad about you,
More lost without you.
And so it goes...

Can you imagine
How much I'll love you,
The more I see you,
As years go by?
I know the only one for me
Can only be you.
My arms won't free you,
My heart won't try.

I know the only one for me
Can only be you.
My arms won't free you,
My heart won't try. ·

Words by Mack Gordon, Music by Harry Warren

THE VOWS GO UNBROKEN
(Always True to You)

From the moment I met you,
You made my life complete.
This wave of pure emotion
Has swept me off my feet.

And tonight when we kissed,
You still took my breath away.
It goes without saying,
But I'll say it anyway.

The vows go unbroken
And you still know I do.
Love, keep and honor,
Always true to you.

Though I have been tempted,
Oh I have never strayed.
I'd die before I'd damage
This union we have made.

The vows go unbroken
And you still know I do.
Love, keep and honor,
Always true to you.

I knew from the first,
For better or worst,
I'd stand by you all my life.
And the vows go unbroken.
And you still know I do.
Love, keep and honor,
Always true to you.
Love, keep and honor,
Always true to you.

Words & Music by Gary Burr and Eric Kaz

THE WAY HE
MAKES ME FEEL

There's no chill and yet I shiver
There's no flame and yet I burn
I'm not sure what I'm afraid of
And yet I'm trembling
There's no storm yet I hear thunder
And I'm breathless why I wonder
Weak one moment then the next I'm fine

I feel as if I'm falling
Every time I close my eyes
And flowing through my body
Is a river of surprise
Feelings are awakening
I hardly recognize as mine

What are all these new sensations
What's the secret they reveal
I'm not sure I understand
But I like the way I feel

Oh why why why why oh

Why is it that every time
I close my eyes he's there
The water shining on his skin,
The sunlight in his hair
And all the while I'm thinking things
That I can't wait to share with him

I'm a bundle of confusion
Yet it has a strange appeal
Did it all begin with him
And the way he makes me feel
I like the way he makes me feel, he makes me feel,
I like the way, I like the way he makes me feel.

Words by Alan and Marilyn Bergman,
Music by Michel Legrand

The Way You Look Tonight

Some day, when I'm awfully low,
When the world is cold,
I will feel a glow just thinking of you...
And the way you look tonight.

Yes you're lovely, with your smile so warm
And your cheeks so soft,
There is nothing for me but to love you,
And the way you look tonight.

With each word your tenderness grows,
Tearing my fear apart...
And that laugh that wrinkles your nose,
It touches my foolish heart.

Lovely ... Never, ever change.
Keep that breathless charm.
Won't you please arrange it ?
'Cause I love you ... Just the way you look tonight.

Mm, Mm, Mm, Mm,
Just the way you look tonight.

Words by Dorothy Fields, Music by Jerome Kern

THE WIND BENEATH MY WINGS

It must have been cold there in my shadow,
To never have sunlight on your face.
You've been content to let me shine,
You always walked a step behind.

I was the one with all the glory,
While you were the one with all the strength...
Only a face without a name.
I never once heard you complain.

It might have appeared to go unnoticed,
But I've got it all here in my heart.
I want you to know I know the truth:
I would be nothing without you.

Did you ever know that you're my hero?
And everything I would like to be?
I can fly higher than an eagle,
'Cause you are the wind beneath my wings.

Words & Music by Larry Henley and Jeff Silbar

THEME FROM ICE CASTLES
(Through the Eyes of Love)

Please, don't let this feeling end.
It's everything I am,
Everything I want to be.
I can see what's mine now
Finding out what's true,
Since I found you
Looking through the eyes of love.

And now I can take the time.
I can see my life
As it comes up shining now.
Reaching out to touch you
I can feel so much
Since I found you
Looking through the eyes of love.

And now
I do believe
That even in the storm we'll find some light.
Knowing you're beside me
I'm all right.

Please, don't let this feeling end.
It might not come again and I want to remember.
How it feels to touch you,
How I feel so much
Since I found you
Looking through the eyes of love.

Words by Carole Bayer Sager, Music by Marvin Hamlisch

THIS EVERYDAY LOVE

Can't get enough of this everyday love
Can't get enough of this everyday love

Each morning the sun shines through my window
Lands on the face of a dream come true
I shuffle to the kitchen for my coffee
And catch up on the front page morning news
Then she walks up behind me and
throws her arms around my neck
Just another normal thing I've come to expect

Chorus:
It's ordinary plain and simple
Typical, this everyday love
Same 'ol, same 'ol keeping it new
(Same 'ol/This everyday love)
Emotional, so familiar
Nothing about it too peculiar
Oh, but I can't get enough
Of this everyday love

Every afternoon I make a phone call
Listen to the voice that warms my heart
I drag myself through a few more hours
Then head on home to try and beat the dark
Her smile will be right there when I step through that door
And it will be there tomorrow, just like everyday before

(Chorus)

Wouldn't change one single thing about it
No, it's run-of-the-mill, still I can't live with-out it

(Chorus)

Yeah, of this everyday love
Can't get enough of this everyday love
Can't get enough of this everyday love
Can't get enough of this everyday love
Can't get enough

Words & Music by Danny Wells and Gene Nelson

This Guy's In
Love With You

You see this guy,
This guy's in love with you.
Yes, I'm in love,
Who looks at you the way I do?
When you smile,
I can tell we know each other very well.
How can I show you I'm glad
I got to know you,
'Cause I need your love.
I want your love.
Say you're in love,
In love with this guy.
If not I'll just die.

I've heard some talk,
They say you think I'm fine.
This guy's in love,
And what I'd do to make you mine.
Tell me now, is it so?
Don't let me be the last to know.

My hands are shaking,
Don't let my heart keep breaking,
'Cause I need you love.
I want your love.
Say you're in love,
In love with this guy.
If not I'll just die.

Words by Hal David, Music by Burt Bacharach

Timber, I'm Falling In Love

Right time, the right place
The right body, the right face
Timber I'm falling in love

It started slow, it's coming fast
I got a feelin' it's gonna last
Timber I'm falling in love

You're so pretty, look so sweet
Your love's sweepin' me off of my feet
You're the only one I'm dreamin' of
I can't believe that I'm falling in love

Who knows how love starts
I woke up with you in my heart
Timber I'm falling in love

You're so pretty, look so sweet
Your love's sweepin' me off of my feet
You're the only one I'm dreamin' of
I can't believe that I'm falling in love

Timber I'm falling in love
Timber I'm falling in love
Timber I'm falling in love

Words & Music by Kostas Lazarides

To Me

To me,
You are the hand that I reach for
When I've lost my way.
To me, you are the first star of evening,
The sun that warms my day.
Just as sure as I'm sure there's a heaven,
This was meant to be.
No road is too long as long as you belong to me.

To me,
You are the truth I believe in;
I believe in you.
To me, you are the love I have looked for
My whole life through.
Just as sure as I'm sure there's a heaven,
This was meant to be.
No road is too long as long as you belong to me.

Just as sure as I'm sure there's a heaven,
This was meant to be.
No road is too long as long as you belong to me.

Words & Music by Mack Davis and Mike Reid

We've Only Just Begun

We've only just begun to live, white lace and promises
A kiss for luck and we're on our way
(we've only begun)
Before the risin' sun we fly, so many roads to choose
We start out walkin' and learn to run
(and yes we've just begun)

Sharin' horizons that are new to us
Watchin' the signs along the way
Talkin' it over just the two of us
Workin' together day to day (together)

And when the evenin' comes, we smile,
so much of life ahead
We'll find a place where there's room to grow
(And yes we've just begun)

Sharin' horizons that are new to us
Watchin' the signs along the way
Talkin' it over just the two of us
Workin' together day to day (together, together)

And when the evenin' comes, we smile,
so much of life ahead
We'll find a place where there's room to grow
And yes we've just begun

Words & Music by Roger Nichols and Paul Williams

WHAT ARE YOU DOING FOR THE REST OF YOUR LIFE?

What are you doing the rest of your life;
North and south and east and west of your life?
I have only one request of your life,
That you spent it all with me.

All the seasons and the times of your days,
All the nickels and the dimes of your days.
Let the reasons and the rhymes of your days
All begin and end with me.

I want to see your face in every kind of light;
In fields of dawn and forests of the night;
And when you stand before the candles on a cake,
Oh, let me be the one to hear the silent wish you make.

Those tomorrows waiting deep in your eyes,
In the world of love you keep in your eyes.
I'll awaken what's asleep in your eyes.
It may take a kiss or two.

Through all of my life,
Summer, winter, spring and fall of my life,
All I ever will recall of my life
Is all of my life with you.

Words by Alan and Marilyn Bergman,
Music by Michel Legrand

When A Man Loves A Woman

When a man loves a woman,
Can't keep his mind on nothin' else,
He'll trade the world for the good thing he found.
If she's bad, he can't see it,
She can do no wrong,
Turn his back on his best friend if he put her down.

When a man loves a woman,
He'll spend his very last dime,
Tryin' to hold on to what he needs.
He'll give up all his comforts,
Sleep out in the rain,
If she says that's how it's gonna be.

When a man loves a woman,
Give up everything he has,
Try to hold on to her precious love.
Baby, please don't treat me bad.

When a man loves a woman,
Down deep in his soul,
She can bring him such misery.
If she's playing him for a fool,
He's the last one to know,
Lovin' eyes don't ever see.

When a man loves a woman,
Give up everything he has,
Try to hold on to her previous love.
Baby, please don't treat me bad.

Words & Music by Calvin Lewis and Andrew Wright

WHEN I FALL IN LOVE

When I fall in love,
It will be forever,
Or I'll never fall in love.
In a restless world like this is,
Love is ended before it's begun
And too many moonlight kisses
Seem to cool in the warmth of the sun.

When I give my heart,
It will be completely,
Or I'll never give my heart.
And the moment
I can feel that
You feel that way, too.
Is when I fall in love with you.

Words & Music by Edward Heman and Victor Young

WHEN I SAID I DO

These times are troubled and these times are good,
And they're always gonna be.
They rise and they fall.
We take 'em all that we should.
Together, you and me,
Forsaking them all.
Deep in the night and by the light of day,
It always looks the same.
True love always does.
And here by your side,
We're a million miles away.
Nothing's ever gonna change the way I feel.
The way it is is the way that it was.
When I said I do, I meant that I will,
'Til the end of all time,
Be faithful and true,
Devoted to you.
That's what I had in mind
When I said I do.

Well, this old world keeps changin'
And the world stays the same
For all who came before.
And it goes hand in hand,
Only you and I can undo
All that we became.
That makes us so much more
Than a woman and a man
And after everything that comes and goes around
Has only passed us by,
Here alone in our dreams,
I know there's a lonely heart in every lost and found.
But forever you and I will be the ones
Who found out what forever means.

Words & Music by Clint Black

YEARS FROM HERE

Standing here face to face,
I feel my heart overflowing with love and emotion.
The moment you took my hand,
There was no doubt in my mind about our future.
I don't need a crystal ball,
Through your eyes I see it all.

Years from here,
We'll look back and treasure this moment forever
inside our hearts.
And from here to there,
We'll make a million memories that we can share
Years from here.

I can promise you this
With every breath I take, I'll live to love you.
I'll go above and beyond
To give you everything that one man can give you.
I know we've just begun
And the best is still yet to come.

Years from here,
We'll look back and treasure this moment forever inside our hearts.
And from here to there,
We'll make a million memories that we can share
Years from here.

Words & Music by
Gary Baker, Jerry Williams, and Frank J Myers

You Are
So Beautiful

You are so beautiful
To me
You are so beautiful
To me
Can't you see
You're everything I hope for
You're everything I need
You are so beautiful to me

You are so beautiful
To me
You are so beautiful
To me
Can't you see
You're everything I hope for
You're every, everything I need
You are so beautiful to me

Words & Music by Billy Preston and Bruce Fisher

YOU GIVE GOOD LOVE

I found out what I've been missing
Always on the run
I've been looking for someone
Now you're here like you've been before
And you know just what I need
It took some time for me to see that...

Chorus:
You give good love to me
To me baby
So good take this heart into your hands
You give good love to me
Never too much will never be
Baby you give good love

Never stopping, I was always searching
For that perfect love
The kind that girls like me dream of
Now you're here like you've been before
And you know just what I need
It took some time for me to see that

(Chorus)

Never too much will never be
Baby you give good love

Never, can't stop looking around
It's not what this love's all about
Our love is here to stay, to stay

Baby, You give good love

You give good love to me
To me baby

So good take this heart into your hands
You give good love to me
Never too much will never be
Baby you give good love

Words & Music by La Forrest Cope

You Light Up My Life

So many nights
I'd sit by my window
Waiting for someone
To sing me his song.
So many dreams
I kept deep inside me,
Alone in the dark,
But now you've come along.

And you light up my life.
You give me hope,
To carry on.
You light up my days
And fill my nights with song.

Rollin' at sea,
Adrift on the waters,
Could it be finally
I'm turning for home.
Finally a chance
To say, "Hey! I love you."
Never again
To be all alone.

And you light up my life.
You give me hope,
To carry on.
You light up my days
And fill my nights with song.

You light up my life.
You give me hope,
To carry on.
You light up my days
And fill my nights with song.
It can't be wrong
When it feels so right,
'Cause you
You light up my life.

Words & Music by Joe Brooks

YOUR SONG

It's a little bit funny this feeling inside
I'm not one of those who can easily hide
I don't have much money, but boy if I did,
I'd buy a big house where we both could live

If I was a sculptor, but then again, no
Or a man who makes potions in a travelling show
I know it's not much, but it's the best I can do
My gift is my song and this one's for you

And you can tell everybody this is your song
It may be quite simple but now that it's done
I hope you don't mind,
I hope you don't mind that I put down in words
How wonderful life is while you're in the world

I sat on the roof and kicked off the moss
Well a few of the verses well they've got me quite cross
But the sun's been quite kind while I wrote this song
It's for people like you that keep it turned on

So excuse me forgetting but these things I do
You see I've forgotten if they're green or they're blue
Anyway the thing is what I really mean
Yours are the sweetest eyes I've ever seen

Words by Bernie Taupin, Music by Elton John

You're Still The One

When I first saw you, I saw love.
And the first time you touched me, I felt love.
And after all this time, you're still the one I love.

Looks like we made it
Look how far we've come my baby
We mighta took the long way
We knew we'd get there someday

They said, "I bet they'll never make it"
But just look at us holding on
We're still together still going strong

Chorus:
(Still the one)   Still the one I run to
The one that I belong to
Still the one I want for life
(Still the one)   Still the one that I love
The only one I dream of
Still the one I kiss good night

Ain't nothin' better
We beat the odds together
I'm glad we didn't listen
Look at what we would be missin'

They said, "I bet they'll never make it"
But just look at us holding on
We're still together still going strong

(Chorus 2x)

I'm so glad we made it
Look how far we've come my baby

Words & Music by Shania Twain and Mutt Lange

You're The Inspiration

You know our love was meant to be
The kind of love to last forever;
And I want you here with me
From tonight until the end of time.
You should know everywhere I go,
Always on my mind, in my heart, in my soul, baby.

You're the meaning of my life,
You're the inspiration.
You bring meaning to my life,
You're the inspiration.
Want to have you near me,
I want to have you near me
Saying no one needs you more than I need you.

And I know it's plain to see
We're so in love when we're together;
And I need you here with me
From tonight until the end of time.
You should know, everywhere I go,
Always on my mind, in my heart, in my soul, baby.

Words & Music by David Foster and Peter Cetera

(You've Got)
PERSONALITY

Oh-oh-over and over
I'll prove my love to you
Over and over, what more can I do
Over and over, my friends say I'm a fool
But oh-oh-over and over
I'll be a fool for you

'Cause you've got - (personality)
Walk - (personality) talk - (personality)
Smile - (personality) charm - (personality)
Love - (personality)

'Cause you got a great big heart
Well over -and over
I'll be a fool for you
Well, well, well over and over
What more can I do

Oh-oh-oh-oh-oh-over and over
I said that I loved you
Over and over, honey now it's the truth
Over and over, my friends say that I'm a fool
But oh-oh-over and over
I'll be a fool for you

Words & Music by Lloyd Price and Harold Logan

Our Favorite Songs

The following lyrics reproduced in this book are reprinted by permission from
UNIVERSAL MUSIC PUBLISHING GROUP, Los Angeles, CA 90064-1712.

- AFTER ALL (Love Theme from CHANCES ARE), by Dean Pitchford and Tom Snow. © 1989 EMI TRIPLE STAR MUSIC, INC., SNOW MUSIC and PITCH FORD MUSIC.

- ALL I DO IS DREAM OF YOU, by Arthur Freed and Nacio Herb Brown. © 1934 (Renewed) Metro-Goldwyn-Mayer Inc. All Rights controlled by EMI Robbins Catalog Inc. All Rights controlled by EMI Robbins Catalog Inc.

- ALL I EVER NEED IS YOU, by Jimmy Holiday and Eddie Reeves. © 1970, 1971 (Copyrights renewed) EMI U CATALOG INC. and RACER MUSIC, INC. All Rights Controlled by EMI U CATALOG INC. (Publishing).

- ALL I HAVE, by Beth Nielsen Chapman and Eric Kaz. © 1990, 1991 WB Music Corp., Macy Place Music and Zena Music. All rights on behalf of MACY PLACE MUSIC administered by WB MUSIC CORP.

- ALL THE MAN THAT I NEED, by Dean Pitchford and Michael Gore. © 1990, 1991 WARNER-TAMERLANE PUBLISHING CORP. BODY ELECTRIC MUSIC and FIFTH OF MARCH MUSIC. All Rights on behalf of BODY ELECTRIC MUSIC Administered by WARNER-TAMERLANE PUBLISHING CORP.

- ALWAYS, by Jonathan Lewis, Wayne Lewis and David Lewis. © 1983 WB Music Corp. and Jodaway Music. All Rights Administered by WB MUSIC CORP.

- AMAZED, by Marv Green, Aimee Mayo, Chris Lindsey. ©1999 Warner-Tamerlane Publishing Corp., Golden Wheat Music, Careers-BMG Music Publishing & Songs Of Nashville Dreamworks. All Rights o/b/o Golden Wheat Music administered by Warner-Tamerlane Publishing Corp.

- BECAUSE YOU LOVED ME, by Diane Warren. © 1996 Realsongs and Touchstone Pictures Songs & Music.

- COMPLETELY, by Diane Warren. © 1993 Realsongs

- EBB TIDE, by Carl Sigman and Robert Maxwell. © 1953 (Renewed) EMI Robbins Catalog Inc. © 1953 (Renewed 1981) EMI ROBBINS CATALOG INC.

- ENDLESS LOVE, by Lionel Richie. © 1981 PGP MUSIC and BROCKMAN MUSIC. All Rights in the U.S. Administered by WB MUSIC CORP. and elsewhere throughout the world by INTERSONG-USA, INC.

- (EVERYTHING I DO) I DO IT FOR YOU, by Bryan Adams, Robert John Lange and Michael Kamen. © 1991 Zachary Creek Music, Inc., Miracle Creek Music, Inc., Almo Music Corp.,Badams Music and Zomba Publishing.

- EVERYTHING I HAVE IS YOURS, by Harold Adamson and Burton Lane. © 1933 (Renewed) Metro-Goldwyn-Mayer Inc. Rights for the Extended Renewal Term in the United States controlled by CHAPPELL & CO. and EMI ROBBINS CATALOG INC. Rights outside the United States Administered by EMI ROB BINS CATALOG INC. (Publishing) and WARNER BROS. PUBLICATIONS U.S. INC. (Print).

- FOR YOU I WILL, by Diane Warren. © 1996 REALSONGS/WB MUSIC CORP. (ASCAP).

- FROM THIS MOMENT ON, by Shania Twain and R. J. Lange. © 1997 Universal - Songs of PolyGram International, Inc./Loon Echo Inc. (BMI)and Out Of Pocket Productions Ltd. All Rights o/b/o Out Of Pocket Productions Ltd. controlled by Zomba Enterprises Inc. (ASCAP) for the U.S. and Canada.

- HAVE YOU EVER REALLY LOVED A WOMAN, by Bryan Adams, Robert John "Mutt" Lange and Michael Kamen. © 1995 Badams Music Limited, Out Of Pocket Productions Limited, K-Man Music Corp., New Line Music Co. and Sony Songs Inc. All Rights o/b/o Out Of Pocket Productions Limited controlled by Zomba Enterprises for the U.S. and Canada.

- I BELIEVE IN YOU AND ME, by Sandy Linzer and David Wolfert. © 1981, 1982 Linzer Music Company, Charles Koppelman Music, Martin Bandier Music and Jonathan Three Music.

- I CAN'T BEGIN TO TELL YOU, by Mack Gordon and James V. Monaco. © 1945 (Renewed) WB Music Corp.

- I CROSS MY HEART, by Steve Dorff and Eric Kaz. © 1990 Warnerbuilt Songs, Inc., Dorff Songs and Zena Music. All Rights on behalf of Dorff Songs Administered by WARNERBUILT SONGS, INC.

- I FINALLY FOUND SOMEONE, by Barbra Streisand, Marvin Hamlisch, R. J. Lange and Bryan Adams. © 1996, 1997 Out of Pocket Productions Ltd. (All Rights Controlled by Zomba Enterprises Inc. for the U.S. and Canada)/Badams Music ltd./Emanuel Music and TSP Music, Inc. All Rights on behalf of Badams Music Ltd., Emanuel Music and TSP Music Inc. Administered by Sony/ATV Publishing.

- I ONLY HAVE EYES FOR YOU, by Al Dubin and Harry Warren. © 1934 WARNER BROS. INC. (Renewed).

- I SWEAR, by Gary Baker and Frank Myers. © 1993 Rick Hall Music, Inc. and Morganactive Songs, Inc.

- IF YOU ASKED ME TO, by Diane Warren. © 1989, 1990 REALSONGS and UA MUSIC INC. Rights on behalf of UA MUSIC INC. controlled and administered by EMI APRIL MUSIC INC.

- IF YOU SAY MY EYES ARE BEAUTIFUL, by Elliot Willensky. © 1985 Music Center/Black Stallion Music.

- LOVE AND MARRIAGE, by Sammy Cahn and James Van Heusen. © 1955 by Barton Music Corp. Copyright Renewed and Assigned to Barton Music Corp. and Cahn Music Company. All Rights on behalf of Cahn Music Company administered by WB MUSIC CORP.

- LOVE IS A MANY SPLENDORED THING, by Paul Francis Webster and Sammy Fain. © 1955 TWENTIETH CENTURY MUSIC CORPORATION. © Renewed 1983 EMI MILLER CATALOG INC.

- LOVE LIKE OURS, by Alan Bergman, Marilyn Bergman, Dave Grusin. © 1999 Threesome Music (ASCAP) & Raw Deal Music (ASCAP). All Rights o/b/o Threesome Music administered by WB Music Corp.

- LOVE, ME, by Skip Ewing and Max T. Barnes. © 1991 Acuff-Rose Music, Inc., Warner Bros. Music Corp. and Two Sons Music.

- MAKIN' WHOOPEE, by Gus Kahn and Walter Donaldson. © 1928 (Renewed) WB MUSIC CORP. Rights for the Extended Term in the U.S. Assigned to Gilbert Keyes Music and Donaldson Publishing.

- MISTY, by Johnny Burke and Erroll Garner. © 1954, 1955 (Copyrights Renewed) Reganesque Music, Marke Music Publishing Co., Inc., Limerick Music Corp., Timo-Co Music & Octave Music Publishing.

- NOW AND FOREVER (You And Me), by David Foster, Jim Vallance and Randy Goodrum. © 1986 Air Bear Music, Irving Music Inc., Calypso Toonz and California Phase.

- STAND BY YOUR MAN, by Tammy Wynette and Billy Sherrill. © 1968 (Renewed) EMI Gallico Music Corp.

- SUNRISE, SUNSET, by Sheldon Harnick and Jerry Bock. © 1964 (Renewed 1992) Mayerling Productions Ltd. and Jerry Bock Enterprises.

- THE BEST YEARS OF MY LIFE, by Stephen Allen Davis, Will Jennings. © 1993 Warner-Tamerlane Publishing Corp., Original Twangstar Music, Will And David Music, Blue Sky Rider Songs. All Rights o/b/o Original Twangstar Music administered by Warner-Tamerlane Publishing Corp.

- THE GREATEST LOVE OF ALL, by Linda Creed and Michael Masser. © 1977 EMI Gold Horizon Music Corp. and EMI Golden Torch Music Corp.

- THE MORE I SEE YOU, by Mack Gordon and Harry Warren. © 1945 (Renewed) WB MUSIC CORP.

- THE VOWS GO UNBROKEN (Always True To You), by Gary Burr and Eric Kaz. © 1988 Gary Burr Music and Zena Music.

- THE WAY HE MAKES ME FEEL, by Alan and Marilyn Bergman and Michel Legrand. © 1983 Emanuel Music, Threesome Music Co., Ennes Productions Ltd. All Rights throughout the World Administered by EMI APRIL MUSIC INC. (Publishing) and WARNER BROS. PUBLICATIONS U.S. INC. (Print.)

- THE WIND BENEATH MY WINGS, by Larry Henley and Jeff Silbar. © 1982 Warner House Of Music & WB Gold Music Corp.

- THEME FROM ICE CASTLES ("Through The Eyes Of Love"), by Carole Bayer Sager and Marvin Hamlisch. © 1978 EMI Gold Horizon Music Corp. and EMI Golden Torch Music Corp.

- THIS GUY'S IN LOVE WITH YOU, by Burt Bacharach and Hal David. © 1968 (Renewed) New Hidden Valley Music & Casa David Music. All Rights o/b/o New Hidden Valley Music administered by WB Music Corp.

- TO ME, by Mack Davis and Mike Reid. © 1982 Acuff-Rose Music, Inc. and Lodge Hall Music, Inc.

- WHAT ARE YOU DOING THE REST OF YOUR LIFE?, by Alan and Marilyn Bergman and Michel Legrand. © 1969 (Renewed) United Artists Music Company, Inc. All Rights Controlled by EMI U CATALOG INC. (Publishing) and WARNER BROS. PUBLICATIONS U.S. INC. (Print).

- WHEN A MAN LOVES A WOMAN, by Calvin Lewis and Andrew Wright. © 1966 (Renewed) Pronto Music, Inc. and Quinvy Music Pub. Co. All Rights Administered by WARNER-TAMERLANE PUBLISHING CORP.

- WHEN I FALL IN LOVE, by Edward Heyman and Victor Young. © 1952 (Renewed) Chappell & Co. and Intersong-USA, Inc.

- WHEN I SAID I DO, by Clint Black. © 1999 Blackened Music (BMI). All Rights o/b/o Blackened Music administered by Warner-Tamerlane Publishing Corp.

- YEARS FROM HERE, by Gary Baker, Jerry Williams and Frank J. Myers. © 1995 Zomba Enterprises Inc./Zomba Songs Inc./Dixie Stars Music.

- YOU LIGHT UP MY LIFE, by Joe Brooks. © 1976 Curb Songs/Universal - PolyGram International Publishing.

- YOU'RE STILL THE ONE, by Shania Twain and R.J. Lange. © 1997 Universal - Songs of PolyGram International Inc., Loon Echo Inc. (BMI) and Out Of Pocket Productions Ltd. All Rights on behalf of Out Of Pocket Productions Ltd. controlled by Zomba Enterprises Inc. (ASCAP) for the U.S. and Canada.

- YOU'RE THE INSPIRATION, by David Foster and Peter Cetera. © 1984 Foster Frees Music, Inc. and Double Virgo Music. All Rights on behalf of Foster Frees Music, Inc. administered by WARNER-TAMERLANE PUBLISHING CORP. (BMI).

Music FOR YOUR *Life Together*

NAXOS

LOOK NO FURTHER THAN NAXOS FOR THE BEST MUSIC SUITED TO EVERY SETTING, WHETHER ROMANTIC AND RELAXING OR ENERGETIC AND STIMULATING.

Classic Christmas

Listen, Learn, and Grow

Romantic Symphonies

Classic Thanksgiving

A-Z of Classical and Opera